Bandits Come and Remove Her Body in the Night

Also by Toni Thomas:

Chosen	Brick Road Poetry Press
Fast as Lightening	Gribble Press
Walking on Water	Finishing Line Press
Blue Halo	Annalese Press
Ace Raider of the Unfathomable Universe	Annalese Press
You'll be Fast as Lightning Coveting my Painted Tail	Annalese Press
Hotsy Totsy Ballroom	Annalese Press
Love Adrift in the City of Stars	Annalese Press
In the Pink Arms of the City	Annalese Press
In the Kingdom of Longing	Annalese Press
The Things We Don't Know	Annalese Press
In the Boarding House for Unclaimed Girls	Annalese Press
They Became Wing Perfect and Flew	Annalese Press
Unburdened Kisses	Annalese Press
There is This	Annalese Press
Here	Annalese Press

Bandits Come and Remove Her Body in the Night

Poems

First published in 2023 by Annalese Press
134 Towngate
Netherthong
Holmfirth
West Yorkshire HD9 3XZ
England

Cover design and layout by Peter Wadsworth
Cover drawing: Mary Cassatt
Mimi as a Brunette, ca. 1889

British Library Cataloguing-in-Publication Data
A catalogue record for this book is available on
request from the British Library.

ISBN 978-1-7394457-1-3

I know there is someone
looking for me day and night inside her hand,
and coming upon me, each moment, in her shoes.
Doesn't she know the night is buried
with spurs behind the kitchen?

I know there is someone composed of my pieces,
whom I complete when my waist
goes galloping on her precise little stone.
Doesn't she know that money once out for her likeness
never returns to her trunk?

I know the day,
but the sun has escaped from me.

Cesar Vallejo

Translated by James Wright and Robert Bly

CONTENTS

PART THREE   *The Cataclysmic Worship of Roses*

PART FOUR   *You Preempt God, Build a Fortress in My Imagination*

PART FIVE   *Ordinary as Moth Wings*

A Child's Verse

Sally Pudding says
Fix Me   Fix Me   Fix Me
and I tell her she's alright
but she's not alright
and in the midst of the gale
we see God devouring her clover
red as sin
red as the ruby bracelets she wears
up her arm

and after the gale
which is long and protracted
nothing remains
except this field
and God
who races around still
with all his pejoratives
his terrible loose tongue raging.

PART ONE
I Parenthesis Want
Behind a Barbed Wire Fence

The World's Hypnotic Aerial Heart Gloating

Maybe it will come back to me
the night with its diagnostic wheels
missives of happiness that wear cleats
vanquish the moon's sweet tongue
the dialysis machine
the palm reader dismisses
with her expert hands.

You wore the silk kimono studded with gardenias
the day the sky eloped
your tea leaves of hope
blue morning teacup
shattered across the parquet.

I stop eating after that
grow pencil thin
don't want to talk about this
don't talk about it for years
the pool of your want that infests me
clings to the room's cramped feet
the way dissolution wraps
my father's blue voice
makes a mockery of justice
low scooped rayon
black beetles squirming to death
inside the sting of his kerosene.

When I become slim enough
you feed me fish hooks to heaven
draw exotic dresses
out of your hat trick days
fashion me as inoffensive as sugar
white cake batter

safe words
with their penitence towing.

It is a miracle what I will do
to drink up your light
become fledgling as the day lily.

I cut out paper angels
identical ones
pin them to my wall
as if there is no tomorrow
no dead mother
girl with her amputated bracelet
amputated life
weeping.

In the Shadow of my Biology Class

you gave me the formula
an imprint in my brain
that dissolves as soon as it is placed there
like sugar dissolves in hot water
marriage melts into a consolation of light bulbs
and what we thought we love turns
stridently away.

Of course in the tissue breathed house
your camisoles live on forever
they are exact and perfect rimmed
in lace filigree, a denial of rain.
I polish my shoes, dine on jasmine
inconsolable roses
tack male screen idols to the wall—
Marlon Brando, James Dean—
imagine black mascara, high heels
stacked as heaven, fur muffs
that keep my hands from freezing
the sleigh an anthem of bells
as it sweeps me over the winter fields
sweeps the gorgeous women with arched brows
perfectly stippled waistlines.
But this is not Siberia.
There are no wolves trailing.
No frostbitten feet.
The tongue of the night devours its shadow.
Perpetual midnight.
Champagne chilled in the dozed glass.

In high school science lab they made us dissect frogs
find the parts beneath their green skin
as if I could understand a being only by severing
piecemeal till nothing was left.

I bribed George R. with his steady impenetrable hands
to manage the steel blade, looked away out the window
into the cottonwoods, the first green of March crooning.

If I take a blade now, all grown up, wield it with a steady hand
will I understand the world better
squeeze out the mysteries that have shuffled like clumsy
undetermined children about my yard
will I be lauded for my surgical mind
the way I've disposed of your body
shrunk your hands into a glass globe
that can be shaken into a snowstorm
but never trundles away
can a camisole hold all the mystery
of the world?

One day I will wake up vacant
as after a storm
or when a car sidewalls you unexpected
and all my decency comes home
from decay.

Does the Starlight Ache

when the morning sky devours
your dark skin
is the girl with the severed arm
able to will it back
the power of some unbrutish determination
to win the world with her song
will I wake one day without
pebbles in my shoes
my long hair no longer a denial
of the efficiency of scissors
the time between now and then
just a remnant of mothering
mated to the wall?

Spring has arrived on tired feet
with its wings heaving.
I stockpile cake batter
white as virgin snow
unhinge my panty hose.
It is May
but the weight of the rain keeps
pawing.

The nuns told us
the obliging and selfless
inherit the world
enjoy predictable meals
wallpaper stippled in ranunculus.

But does anybody ever shred the even pallor
of these walls?

In the Apology of Want

you feel a breeze
forensic
not consolatory as hope
that tired proposition
that sinks concave in bath water
spoons *simple* over the allegory
of the bread

but then maybe some people are
meant to eat like this
the fatted cow breaking
my diminutive cousins with
their thin wafers
as if want has no buttress to play
and you are what you are
what you become
sweet bun with honey
cantankerous sojourn

Parisian tart of a complex experience
self anointed
buffed

in a world of distress
not mauled by tigers
always at home
inebriated with shine.

The Triumph of Baking

Were you palpable in your green dress
last hurrahs that kept the paint peeled
lawn chair anchored to the front yard
to cosmos dangling their beautiful thin bodies
in the July sun?

Is it hard to become invisible at 40
fudge marbled away
as if god holds only a saccharine key
defames wrinkles
turns red faced pollsters into
counting machines
that measure the girth and weight
of what we've become?

I remember the ammunition of cake batter
its smooth white texture
the way it slides down the throat
leaves men scratching for mercy
at someone else's door

remember your siren's body
too good for plain cotton
the elliptical nature of sin
seduction of cake
unrisen in the blue bowl.

How many times will you shrink from this world
rise your lips above the common denomination
of wood spoon
the moon scratching grief outside the window
your terribly sensible life
flapping?

What If I Call Her Winsome

as in some girl from a lost age
who signs her name in the
hieroglyphics of want
unspoken table manners
tears the cellophane of hope
and peers inside?

In the stinkpots of happiness
all manner of idle efficiencies
are feigned by man
you are what you are what you wear
what you do
the shy puddle gets swallowed by the day
children are relegated to glass houses
exiled birds
the banners of happiness become
a perfect pose.

Sister—this is the new world calling.
But somewhere along the line
you looked away.

The Penitentiary of Desire

rears its snowy head.
I proposition my father
to draw mercy out of a thin wick
angle happiness onto the floor
while the afternoon
struts in swelled feet.

Make me a recipe for paradise I beg.

My father's hands have grown spiked
worship the dark
strychnine.

I dig lust out
a serpent with emerald eyes
the sinewy presence
of what's been lost.

Axe Handles

He didn't know what you were talking about-
cerulean landscape
his putty knife filling the holes
your heels that kicked in the screen door
the night you ran from him with
your floating anonymous needs.

They say that chiffon looks best in moonlight
mild weather
that a girl with axe handles on her tongue
can go anywhere
not get the shit knocked out.

Deft gardens.
How many times have your knees buckled under
the weight of us?

They say the container of heaven
is green as sin on a flawless day.

Stay here
he says
as if you can pin down the moon
make it light as chiffon
maud as the sky's muscling.

When the Leaves Brown on the Slender Tree

and the jack o lanterns' faces turn
sharp angles to mush
I think of you winding your
bullets of rain into the earth's salt field
your matchless hand fondling
the territorial nature of time
to snatch what's hard pressed.

In the garden moles burrow a tunnel
gnaw the last heads of carrot
the man with arthritis complains
about stiffness
what he can, cannot do
my father worries about winter
plastic sheet on the windows
the voice of money.

November drags its tail in mud so deep
black boots may not carry us.
I spread a tarp over the sandbox
bag shovels, a castle mold, crab shells
coax them to live through winter
into another spring
dream my father's hands pliable.

I never see the moles
just the hills they've left behind
the stump end of carrots
never see my father's hands touch
your waist
run his long tapered fingers

like haloed candles over
the damp trespass of your body.

It will be a record cold winter.
We will be buried in snow
but we don't know that
tacking our pink insulation
between roof rafters
ramming the stuffed snake
long tailed cat under the door lip.

I will grow up with an aversion to cold
thin sleeved
play my fingers furiously
over blue inked surfaces
invisible keys
clay bodies
afraid if they seize up
they will be damned
like you who strode into winter
with your cursed life
red kimono flaming
or my father who fancied himself
a musician
except for the orphaned nature of his hands.

Your Fingers

are cold as cast iron
segregated from hope
rake the soil of my land
looking for milk ponds
memories' lost tuition
the child with the bent stick
destined to scratch heaven.

In the book of my adventures
I mount a stricken horse
attempt to bring things back
like Lazarus who arrived
from the dead
suffering god.

I am convinced it takes more
than a dowsing stick
to find gold
that death is a journey of minefields
night's ecclesiastical hold
that your body is submerged
bolted to concrete
and to reach you I must be almost invisible
deft as cotton
sinkable as the smallest stone.

I Poll You to See if You are Breathing

It is the last time.
You are feckless in your silk kimono
December and flimsy as you
slide over the snow
scrape off the car windows

have not grown up
never will
your tea cup a broken chapel
on the living room floor
your body still breathing
when the ambulance arrives.

I know you don't want to go out
of the world like this
fleeting as birdsong
a whisper of collapse amidst the
mess of our lives.

I check your pulse
as if my own life depends on it
as if heart attacks are only a warning
against decay
say—*you can't do this*
can't   can't   can't
but you do.

Midnight

you have devoured
the hairnets of the moon
my father goes off in the dark
he wants to travel unencumbered
except for the weight of his shoes.
An anonymous poet once said
in the crucible of heaven all things are equal
which means maybe even my father
can arrive half naked.
How many equations does it take
to create stasis, the syrupy voice
inaugurated by lunchmeat?

You rode out of the house rampant as kerosene
a six pack and one suitcase
the mangled dog towing.
How much prerogative does it take
to wear down the face
mill it to fine powder, impervious?
You used to say *-it is the clever*
who inherit the earth
never saw me as strident enough
tried to prepare me for my eventual fall—
the realization that nothing can't be something
in this covetous place.

I spread peach vanilla into my daydreams
pitchers of water
remember the dog side walled up the road
the neighbor girl with one arm who used to build
parapets to mount the moon
remember how my father said she was weak

would never amount to anything
as if we're only a sum of awards
pocketed coin to be tallied.

When I frost my tongue with
the snow's downfall is it possible
I will become speechless
let the white flakes melt heaven
in my empty places
as if something can become nothing
like an open lid
an eye so pure the trees contain it
the girl with the one arm reaches heaven
her faith more than quicksilver
unequal to the rest?

Who Says the Shattered House
Can't Live Here Anymore?

You can live forever
with a sunken wing.
Sylvia's brother did that
took the leftovers of his life
made a nest
maybe not satin coated
but then how much better is
worsted wool in a snowstorm
and come winter we get plenty of them.
Thirty five years old and he still
hobbles out for walks in the snow.

In August the wasps in our yard
get voracious
will dine on anything - pink salmon
cool-aid, the toothpaste my brother dabs
on the balsa of his rudderless plane.
You spread baby oil
manage to keep the wasps
but not the sun from traveling your body.

I don't tell you the garden is shrinking
clutches loose petals
parched geranium
like my body that will whittle itself
into twigs so hard my father's might
can't snap them with his unimmaculate hands.

White cake batter invades the oven.
We send cupcakes three doors down
to Sylvia and her brother.
They are angel food

deny the inclemency
of the rain.

I paint my hands white
am too young to know
that I won't be able to save you
that no man wants a girl
with crimped wings

still believe God is a field
of parched lemons
slice their bodies in half
suck out the juice.
Bitter as ravens my brother says
after one sip
but what does he know
his tongue is sugar coated
on prickly church sermons
that ransom sin
make it pay.

When you slice through
the night
do you enter the day
or only the screech of crows calling?
I hold a telescope up to the moon
as if lust can speak to me
my lucky coin
a recipe against disaster
unprotected days.

In the Arms of the Hexagon

my mother's eye shadow does not run
her hands are becalmed as epistles
and nobody eats the night
with ravenous claws.

The righteous believe they have a
crystal ball in their heads
turn the wind into wood pigeons
live in big porched, four square houses
with deathless geraniums.
Palsy has many faces.
When my fingers engraved the moon
you drew circles with your pen knife.
Eventually the holes got filled in
by a dim perambula
didn't seem so dissonant
inscrutable anymore.

My mother's silk stockings barely manage
to hike themselves up over her legs.
How many silver bangle bracelets
to rattle heaven
how many cigarette butts to burn down
an end table, consume the past?
Her cigarettes singed holes in the arm chair.
Things smolder before they flame.

One day you will grow up like your father
smashing black beetles to the wall.
I detest fortune tellers
the smug way they aerosol your life.
In Amsterdam the canals turn
steely edged women into water seekers

men no longer travel in glass boats
the girl with the ragged tulle clutches tulips
is followed by children
opens envelopes with paper cranes.

Sometimes I sound like Scarlett O'Hara -
but where will I go, what will I do?
nobody answers.
I watch people in the supermarket
their mouths pressed to cell phones
confirmation of the chatty, robust
lives they lead.
My heart is a mute string
on a swollen branch
an invisible flutter of sparrows
paucity of axed ranunculus
in an inked tray.

You want the shoe to fit
the four square house
parasitical morning with its
terminal wires trailing
as if the ambitionless foot
squires nothing of a throne
and the meadow is just plastic wrap
spray painted green
a time-sequenced foray
like this or that
she loves me
she loves me not
each daisy beheaded
petal by petal
till only the plucked
clean center remains.

PART TWO
My Mother Swallows the
Snowy Plover

You Refuse to Buckle Up

live on a knife edge
low cut dresses, bare feet.
Your tattooed arm sports a heart
with its center broken.

She drives like a banshee
my brother says.
It is summer
the paint on our house peeled
the beach a long arm of road away.

You say -*buckle your seat belts*
swerve in traffic
bait the wind with your hair
look woozy in your pastel dress
threaten to float out the window
leave us tethered
to the mercy of the road.

Back then I wanted to chain down
everything that I loved –
the dog, my paint set
brother's pudgy hands
my parents' uneven marriage
chain your voracious body
its need to be elsewhere
till you were ordinary
ironing cotton
lathing jam on the sandwiches
like other mothers
so terribly even
calm.

Some Things Never Say Goodbye

The nasturtiums knock light
out of the sky's loose shoes
fend off the moon
my right eye that has a will of its own
takes on the tallow marks of the world
lives there.
I wonder if any seed can rise to glory
without its thorns?

But we are told to *buckle up*
it's a trip we are on
mama driving in the front seat
my brother gobbling the scenery
the macaroon cookies.
You are not dead yet
handsome with your copper skin
sundress spread paisley
across the vinyl seat.
Many men want you.

At the boat basin off Jones Beach
you unpack ham sandwiches
cool-aid, tubes
swim out further than the rest
become a tiny speck in our blue ocean
scissor the waves slow, deliberate
the way you will depart this life
one bracelet, lost canvas at a time
till only your pale wrists remain.

You Color the Moon

with your red pen
we try to tell you *the moon is white*
our teachers value accuracy
careful observation, a lack of fiction
but you are disinclined toward
an abbreviated imagination
darken the moon till it is red hot
a noxious berry that tempts the girl
in the fairy tale to wander off
into a hushed wood.

Over childhood we become used to your treasons
wobbly handwritten notes to the teacher -
Sadie will be out this morning due to a loose tooth
Nicolas's left foot is aching
when we are painting the yard shed
black and white as a Dalmatian
rubbing glitter dust over the dead roses
dabbing putty between our toes.

Later you will stickpin the moon to your bed
drape it in black chiffon
I will take a flashlight
search the yard, the refrigerator to find you.
The man you married will stockpile
no moist kisses for your bed.
Every day ordinary as cotton
placid lunch meat
your metal tipped shoes clicking.

For a Moment You Triumph Over the Past

make an altar of moonlight.
I am ten years old
it is scary to see you
swaying your hips in the slinky rayon
among the hibiscus
peonies flounced in fuchsia
loud as your lips.
The moon strikes a poise
the night flames
my father tries to etch Orion
onto his palm with a black pen
fails, slams the door
says *stay inside.*

It is fretful watching you
sway across the yard
sing that Peggy Lee tune
I'll be seeing you...
as if a kite has been torn loose
from the fence
my father has turned alien
sealed the house in cellophane
afraid to admit this dark haired
sun bronzed woman back in
with her big voice.

He Left You There, Deserted in Paradise

you take a crow's nest for your bed
it's not perfect
worrisome really
the hours of imposed desertion
housebound with lunch boxes
clotheslines, sick children
your canvases crammed into a corner
of the basement.
That winter you paint the parlor walls black
insist my brother and I eat all our meals
dangling off the side of your bed.
We search the window, the beggar sky
for the bigger one
you say we were made for.

I devise rickshaws with fancy wheels
skies that don't bust
devour white hymns
write your name in the dust
in the yard dirt, blades of rain
scavenge the satin, cake batter
inside your late night weeping
want you to dig a garden out of the earth's grey silt
find the goose that lays
the palpable egg
golden even—
in a climate of disease—
something round
fecund
sublime.

It is Pitch-black

you want to conquer the room's thrifty
while the house tries to sleep
is drifting off into a pallor of unclipped shirts
rhythmic wallpaper.

It is midnight
time when all good things
languish in repose
when your carpetbagger arms
burn cigarettes
torch stars into the room's
qualified landscape.
Nothing escapes
the scour of your wide paintbrush
that wields black
crucifies the walls.

We look on stunned as you mount
dismount the ladder
ignore my father's shrew tongue
hobble our world into another
kind of scenery
black as the dead weight of crow
charred clotheslines
black as the once and for all way
you erase the room's petted light
catacomb want
opaque it
your invincible eye gleaming.

You Wear Sage Musk

silk stockings pulled snug
up over your legs
the rarefied air
everybody muddling
in everybody else's business

pick your name from a squat catalog
pin on the tag
but the lines date you.
There are forests of misshaped shoes
a forked tongue
words with no roots.

The crowd never notices
your drop dead soliloquies.
Someone claims - *to speak is to make power
a spark of your own being.*
You turn sullen after that.

It is cold.
If a girl is not careful
she could lose her satin muff
her third eye
life here.

You Clear Rubble from the Trees

inflate the pink giraffe
sit in your low cut sand chair
till puddles dry up
the plastic flamingo threatens to tango

your jukebox playing
fever when you kiss me.....
fever when you hold me tight...
like a promise to war vets
a banner against dissolution
your polka dot dress pawing.

Give me a light you say
lips snug around the white
sheathed tobacco
as if dying is meant
to be a work of art
white coated
magnanimous even.

You hug our neighbors
feed the tabby cat that scratched
a history of red grooves up your arm
feed my dispassionate father
more than the orphaned nothing
on which he was raised.

You Make a Eulogy out of Bed Bugs

dig a hole
press our yard dirt in pink linen
petals of daisy
the myopic seasons of the world
that burn and rage
lie down in a tame grave.

We sing poverty into the night air
rattle the roof tiles
jangle our cheap bracelets
let god know
we exist
amid the disused shoes
infirmary of bed bugs
happy machinery
that grinds faith down
slow into rust.

You Build an Ark

tell us we can sail anywhere -
the Caribbean, Tahiti
pink surface of the world's lost tongue
carve a masthead
stencil a canopy
for when the wind lashes
the sea churls.

We imagine ourselves roped to you
determined to stay with the ship
you the once lifeguard
strong swimmer
imagine you will always be here
not tethered to my father's thudding rudder
or dead from heart failure
but here in the ark
your muscled body
guiding us effortless
through every storm.

It is Sunday

we anoint our foreheads
with holy water
genuflect at the start of the pews.
At communion you rise up
drop dead glorious with your slinky
rayon dress, spike heels
spangle of bracelets.
Men will crane their necks
as you make your way
down the aisle.

After church service
we stop at Reitmann's Bakery
where you will give us almost anything
and we cram our faces full of crème puff
black and white cookie
as if contrition has its reward
as if we are not just the world's sodden machinery—
are anointed with cake flour
good sugar
consolation for the things
you know
will be taken away.

You Curtain the Bathroom Mirror

scissor yourself out of photograph albums.
What will happen to you now that
those svelte curves have turned ball field?

How do I talk about loss
pebbled shoes
the way loneliness dwarfs the tongue
courage can set up its own brave constituency
stickpin a family
groom the voice
punctuate graveyards?

Over time your body turned traitor.
It was my childhood.
A sadness I watched with a rapt tongue.
But in the sum of a life
are there even more terrible
irrevocable losses
than this one?

You Swallow the Snowy Plover

begin to chirp
spilt feathers
jealous cat
but there's no way to keep you
from unruly then ruling your life.

It was only a matter of time
before his decisive hands
defamed you
blotted out your Liz Taylor looks
into a family of lunch pails

but you have an appetite for happiness
clam digs, beachcombing
low-cut black gowns

swallow the snowy plover
devour it in one fail swoop
before the cat can sink in his claws.
My brother and I look on
watch you chirp in the trees
drizzle emerald over the sidewall
smash a hole in our window
where emptiness longs to be.

You Build a Bridge Between Happiness and Despair

tow rope your life
dangle in midair
your rapacious stockings
burning.

We promise to be everything
firewood and water
blue pagoda, pressed syllables
the painted marionette
forest at midnight
frogs leaping.
This could go on forever—
our uneven chorus
the sanctimonious way life takes hold
then shrivels.

My brother and I attempt to be perfect
impervious to the breakdown of goodness
in a retractable world
become polished as white lightning
genuflect by the bed
turn the other cheek
never get sick
never get married
honor you with our torrid devotion
determination to press death
out of ordinary sheets.

You Fawn Over My Father's Dissonance

make him feel big
pampered as pecans
no long an appendage to
life's armored trust.

The world becomes linen
pressed dress shirts
a solvency of words.

We wiggle and squirm
our way through infinity
as if God is incontestable daylight
the ocean of good fish

guileless woman
in need of nothing
on an ruby sort of day.

You Disavow Madness

tell me St. Jude saves
hairpin your life to my shaved body's
hounded deliverance
go miles in the kitchen to make sure
the cake batter gets nailed
nothing of white angel food
trespasses the fire of my lips.

It is summer.
There are dress sizes so prized
they subterfuge the rain
grow respect like ivy blanketing
a fierce prayer book.

I nibble brussel sprouts, carrots
let not the sin of indulgence
trespass my lips
ride miles over bike trails
as if my body is lightning
unmarred by any maud thing
as if my long hair, twig legs
are a homage to St. Jude
who vouchsafes to protect
umpire the beauty of the world
beyond stadiums
distills our dross into
the fruited field.

You Catalog our Lives

invent fear
because the world isn't fair
and you know it
know our lives can turn crushed lightening
if you don't shelter
map the course of our palpable.

We grow afraid of vagrant cats
afraid to eat contaminated food with my father
at the low end greasy spoon restaurant
afraid of bad report cards
the thorns of roses
way love comes willy nilly
sinks its teeth in then trundles away.

I sleep in the closet of your lament
become implacable – the sickless child
with the sterling grade sheets
measured body, tinsel wings.
My brother crushes chalk
spawns a truck with giant wheels
black walled room
white powdered homilies.

Your death continues to invent fear in us
nothing is pure or sacred
when we erase ourselves slow
one measure at a time
no angel will come to perch
love is a dialog fleeting as sin
and what is meant to be kept
must be anchored
staple gunned into place
vigilant.

In the Book of Beatitudes

you find your freedom
speak in the drunken retinol of hope
where every lost hour an avalanche
of happiness saves
the cross yields to a certain rose.

Wheel barrows of apples invade our yard
melon big as a football stadium
pattypan squash to feed the nation.

We arrive in slippered feet
grow big on the sun's delirium
elbow our way into every corner of garden
till nothing remains hidden
every path holds to its original decency.

In the book of Beatitudes
you marvel at the pallor turned
newborn splendor
bleached white significance
with which we shine.

Everyone Wanted Carnations that Year

droves of them
like an ammunition against pain
so you sunk your teeth
into cosmos, oriental poppies
refused to be pried from their ledge.

It was the year of the crippled summer
consummate rain
the shed in the yard half buckled
the tomato vines a miracle in their
resolution to hold fast to their roots.
I parentheses want
make my face an emblem
of the world's calculated geometry
as if nothing terrible happens
you're not bleeding to death invisibly
inside the four walls, retail job
lunch meat, egg shelled bed.

Agitated summer
the butterfly bush pooled with rain
your soaked sojourns to stake
the lilies back up with your bamboo poles
as if you were bred for rescuing
your cursed mary immaculate body
a drift of sheen.

PART THREE
The Cataclysmic Worship of Roses

Midnight Hairpins My Mother's Hard Shoes

sanctifies time
makes the lobelia bend
to its lost constituencies.

In the cramped house
happiness is polished as a cook stove
you drift in white robes
call nothing out of the yard's machinery
the wallpaper's ceremonial roses.

I tell you it is unseasonable
to live life like this
bowed down to every lost thing
the side-long glances of men
suicidal in their dismay
that midnight and morning
look not dissimilar
in the right hands.

But the day never becomes itself
you almost phantasmagorical
in your soft slippers
terrible order of things
the cataclysmic worship of the roses
their rouged faces
damp with ruin
amid the wallpaper's refrain.

The Epistle of Happiness

blinds my mother to the day's angular light
till she can't see
exiles black birds
grows a picket fence

becomes vague
set in her mud stained feet
surrounded by the bees thrumming
the epistles of heaven
that send her off to death's door
so many things exhausted
by such lack of breath.

My father looks on
his hands impenetrable
casts an impassive eye over the
world's machinery
embraces the far-sighted vision
to staple facts
seize what is.

You Whitewash Your World

make it stay in place
make love with the past
stickpin it to the wall
like butterflies, deathless
on black velvet mounts
that must anoint their body
with eternity's pitfalls.

No brigade will reach here.
You are heaven with a shaved face.
Clean, sober as cake batter.
My brother and I drown in
your smooth white folds

will never marry
only contemplate children
read the grail
of asphyxiated heaven
with our insides bleeding.

You Wish for Happiness

settle for the world's tutelage.
Can I blame you for this
treading water
making your pact with death
on sodden knees?

Your hands are blue missives
matted to a surplus of clothes
thread the wheels of machinery
till you become clockwork
my father's agreeable left eye
expert and windless as steel shoes.

If there are girders
that rise all the way to heaven
you are looking for the top floor
the glass room with the view
indefatigable moment
repose that comes from just once
capturing paradise
holding it between your polished teeth
till it rings.

You Curse the Man in Your Bed

not for lack of money
but for sheer lack of imagination
the way his card tricks
collapse the moon
send evenly labeled envelopes
where sticky love notes long to be.

Don't get me wrong you still
wear the thin silk kimono
travel barefoot into the sawn off places
arm yourself with Asian tea pots
mother of pearl
carved women from Thailand
awnings that collapse the sun's face
keep you white, blotchless
but for him
no longer hold much hope.

Late afternoon you swim secret
in the blue pool
hand water your poppies
red balled geranium
stroke the flamingo
turn our garden wet and slick
wet and slick
with the sheen of your hose.

You Staple Summer

onto the room's scrubbed face
glue daffodils, sunflowers
their lemon yellow coats that
proposition happiness
with a careful tongue

press your lips to heaven
as if the trellis of dissolution
has spilt over our bed
and every day is a July day
teaming with ladybugs.
No one dies in this world
commits adultery
ends up trampled to death
tattooed with an eating disorder
a shattered marriage
cardboard house.

I tease winter to come
drag it secretly into my room
lure it with braised squash
lumpy potato
red sirens
the formidable
lick it, white cake batter
on a blackened tongue
imagine the world before this one
ordinary death
ragged chiffon snagged on branches of moonlight
pitchforks, glue
so many broken toys sighing.

My Mother Prunes the Roses

on her empire waist dress.
It is hard to see her this way
polished teeth
a blue scissor
encyclopedic eye turned into
St. Jude's prayer books
the docile way she calms the man
she has married
dotes on her children
hopes to testify that love is selfless
bypasses the rain.

It is acrimonious
grooming this garden.
I want the foxglove to rise up
devour the sane
her purple flamingo
to spawn relations
stampede the yard.

You Wear Your Empire Waist Dress

bring out a bamboo tray
dessert plates laced with blue pagodas
sweet puffed propositions of your love—
mint wafers, hazelnut cookies, candied pear
petite-fours with their piped rosettes
pink jeweled lips pawing.

Your empire waist dress
holds the sappy yellow of hybrid tulips
looks tight
has shrunk under the sun's harsh gaze.

Day by day
one painted teacup
small mouthful at a time
you work hard to reconstitute heaven
but can paradise really be conjured
with each foil wrapped confection
we lift and lick from this tray?

You Say Goodbye to Your Fake Leopard Muff

don't stickpin it like a voodoo doll
pamper the muff with mothballs
just relinquish it to the basement
to the cargo trunk that holds
black satin dresses, Mexican shawls
rosettes from that other glamorous life in New York
before the anonymous polyester arrived
machine wash warm, tumble dry
the easy care machinery.

Thirty years pass.
I remember my childhood—
the fake leopard muff meant to mimic
the plush of your waltzing
the prize my hands felt being pampered
in such soft folds
the curative nature of sin
my silver spangled mama
succulent, striking
saucy
stepping over every inhospitable thing
conquering her world.

When You Followed Your Pocket Flashlight

into the night
we didn't see you anymore
not for money or silk
the guilt that desertion breeds.
No note left on the side table
declaration of wants
proviso for the conditions on which
you'd return
as if return was a notion
dismissed from the head.

Afterwards we wore sensible pajamas
a stubby prayer book
my brother excavated his left toe
cut his fingernails so short they bled.
In the kitchen every dish turned
disposable
like rootless pigeons
we lived on day old buns
canned ravioli, pizza.

I became the girl with teeth so polished
you can see your face in them
shiny white totems
implacable
even in the rain.

You Fan Midnight

with your serpentine tongue
weren't made this way
coddling death
in the lotus drenched kimono
bowl after bowl of ice cream
the kitchen refrigerator crammed down your throat
gestapo of white enamel
you tyrant of young girls
with sand in their shoes
no corridors left to call home.

Come dark, up on the stepladder
sirens anoint midnight
you paint the parlor walls black
redeem with ornate gold braiding.
One cigarette after another
drops its ash souvenir on the floor.

Someday you will land a garden
of your own making
hum again
the knot of pins slid from your hair
the day's massacres
a sliver of tailgate
pale moon
soothed by your face.

You Drown in Eight Yards of Satin

drape goldfinch, yellow and indigo
over one shoulder
stipple your arm in Indian ink
sacred elephants, an ornate bridge.
Men look at you like a remnant
from another world
copper skinned
your long raven hair silken
but it is no use
none of it will save you.

No man will learn how to tender you
the satin will fade in the sun's clenched fist
you will die alone in a harsh bed
leave a cargo trunk of paintings
duct taped children.
They travel miles
devour cake batter
shoot up white powder
to find some remnant
of your secret burning.

You Hear the Polyphony of the Sky Breathing

unburden your tongue
stop measuring the world
as if night fails
forgive my father his orphaned disposition
forgive the holes in the screen door
cramped three family apartment
drag your web chair onto the lawn
hive with the bees
till nothing, not love or money
will drag you back into the house.
All summer seated in paisley
you pamper the day's lost tongue
stargaze.

In October when the lawn drowns
under a merciless sky
the nasturtiums wilt
you fold up your web chair
let the rain eat you
sopping wet by the yard shed
slinging mud balls
pulverizing heaven
with all your weight.

You Court Disaster

till it finds you
straight pins your past
red shoes.
I call you down from where
the emissaries of light
have missioned your head
till you can't breathe—
heart failure they call it—
I call it the travesty of sin
when a soul is so crushed
it can only contemplate heaven.

Afterwards
my brother and I build an altar
to your name
truss our lives
till prosperity won't find us.
We are purgatory with a blazing head
write poems, sculpt women
run from marriage
porcelain sinks, lunch pails
dig crickets out of a sodden grave.

Fail.
Fail.   Fail.

Invisible in our rubber flippers, rain slicks
insatiable desire to dig you back up
all seasons our garden a death processional
of the supine flowers you once bathed.

Passages

I crossed a bridge
more like a shrunken tower
epistle yet to be written
your hands white as sin
white as the homily of egrets
lounging in the sky's sleep sac.

Cast me your life
you told me
but I was afraid of the devouring
afraid that what's spent
never comes back.
How long could I hold a purse
like this one without breaking
how much cake batter will hold up
the house, the geranium
its gaudy red balls of Christmas
how many wants can sit soiled epistle
in the torn arm of the moon's aching?

I gave you my life
my life
it was no easy thing
to be circled
collapsed
evaporated as water
your hands all over my grave.
In me
a world of forgotten shoes
keeps rattling.

You Took your Wounded Heart

into the world as ice cubes
your grave an epitaph
against dissolution
the purgatory of not spending
what we save.

September comes with its loose tongue
a coronation of leaf fall
the cramped happiness that a
smooth mouth brings.
Cross this bridge he threatened
and you will never come back.
It was a long time ago
before the heart failure
when you contemplated leaving him
boxing the rug, yard toys, stereo.
You will drown in nothing he said.
You couldn't face penniless
two small children, the dogs
beetles in the garden being scalded to death
in the paradise of his kerosene.

Time repeats itself on sodden rails
fields dry up, turn asphalt
faces wax complacent
we grow up
promise never to desert you
later run away to the other side of the world
dine on cake batter
love's capricious
swear we will never let any being
clamp our thin wrists

to a blue prison
trample to death like him.

But it is September
when yard debris gets carted off
and the last of the cosmos hang on
by their beautiful thin throats.
Here on the other side of the country
the ice is no threat
the damp mien of the Northwest's teeth
are polished white as stone
you can cast your life in intractable treasons
recycle the threads
lounge amid the youth driven, clever
accomplished
the comfortable outdoor clothing
impermeable to rain
never look back.

I look back.
See the world buried in tailgates
your red summer dress burning.

PART FOUR
You Preempt God
Build a Fortress in my Imagination

When You Conquer Heaven

will I be the first to see you
in sunlight
unburdening the curtains
adrift in magenta
your abbreviated hems
no longer forlorn
no longer baiting men with
a mint coated breath

but solvent
self possessed even
in a small easy on the eyes way
that denies the obduracy of roses
their thorn flecked faces
wages war on the apostles of plenty
the walled garden of peonies
finds that trace of immigrant sun
marries the day?

You Stumble into Your Future

don't like what you see
a man who lurches but never comes
the tedium of the media's imperatives
dust all over the inlaid mother of pearl
the fury of life
that makes a mockery out of defiant feet
a mockery of loose afternoons
in the wind's cradle.

It will be cold here
you know that
and efficient as those who covet
weedless lawns, punctual dinner plates
children with heads of knowledge, little time.
It will be painful here
you know that
calloused as loose tongues
indifferent side windows
the first will be first
and the last rubbed out with an eraser point
till they have nowhere to shine.
It will be reasonable here
you know that
terribly reasonable
finely tailored as words put through their paces
til the even letters stand anonymous, straight
anchor the truth, spin it.

One day the girl with the bent eye
will walk into nothing
and be gone.
You know that
keep your blue rosary
flaming.

The Tabernacle of Hope

gets torn from God's arms
a lightning bolt
severed away
as the breath of children
stabbed
in February's steel teeth.

Quiet after that
almost frigid
we cast our clear disparaging eye
over the asphalt, cornfields
buttress our words till they come out
even tempered
self determination
chronicles of shine.

Bandits Come and Remove Your Body
in the Night

It is pitch black
your silk comforter crumpled
in a heap on the floor
the kimono's gardenias
sliced in two.

Nothing will be the same.
My father weeps a century of rain
my brother grows up, never marries
never trusts the durability of love
in a crushed can world
I whip cake batter
white as heaven
bowls of it

tell myself loss is just a figment
of some tainted child's imagination
there is nothing evil
in jeopardy in this world
the forsythia will grow back
impale February's snow
the endangered can speak for us
you will lift out of death
arrive home in green shoes

tell myself any girl can climb
the rungs of paradise
spoon by spoon
never depart from this earth
just make herself into a pure
white grave.

One Year the Girl Grew Amnesia

til it took over her mind, her body, her voice
and she couldn't count to ten
train her words to be good girls anymore
and the shoelaces her father insisted on
became loose as cooked spaghetti
loose as her memory of fur rabbits
how to seduce a man
make him love her senseless.
It wasn't long till only the lamppost
in the space between niceness spoke
and her faithful collie, who was after all
her animal twin and trailed her everywhere
into the forgotten.

After that the phone didn't ring
the room whispered garbled secrets.
One day a man knocked on the door
he had ancient hands
a dowsing rod for hunting displaced things
lost rings the ground claims
when the world grows siloed.
They went foraging together—the girl and the man.
She had lost her name
he didn't have one.
She told him the bible story
she'd invented for roses
he gave away his coat.

In March the earth makes a show
of camellias, tulips pregnant with space.
They set the rod to work in the meadow
beyond the sawmill
busted pocket knife, bottle caps
somebody's fish hook, key ring

it startled them
the number of dinked treasures
the dirt rises up.

His forecast was blue sky
and fireflies
she said when her left foot aches
it always means rain.
It rained.
Then the sun came back.

The lamppost kept its one ear
glued to her grate.
The man with no name came back.
Even invisible
in a certain light
in a certain manner of daybreak
this girl could flame.

My Mother Becomes a Scholar but Gets Bored

the logarithms
analysis of light
way philosophy books depict
men's longing to find certainty
the grains of sand lost
in a covetous fist.

Heraclitus, Sophocles, Schopenhauer, Hume
grow thin metaled in the breeze
oriental poppies team their tissue breath
onto the lawn's forgetful.

It is summer.
Bees impregnate the flowers
with their fevered thirst
dozens of tiny spiders spill from a sac
onto the geranium's slant leaves
the dog, cat grow lusty
sprawl their bodies out on concrete
let the sun's loose shoes
tread them.

My mother unties the strict knot
fallen waist length, her long hair
holds the sheen of avocado
glistens amid the cemetery's cold stone.
She forgets sums, precision's halo.
Squirrels chatter in the tree
black flies circle.
No one swats them above the yard table.
Across the duff of earth
my mother sprawls out her body
wide as song.

In the Window of Happiness

my mother turns a blind eye
is fretless of what the neighbors say
has lived long enough to know
her own mind, body's allegiances
damp, dark soil.

Like a Venus flytrap
her petals slay crimson
lure men into her lair.
Outside the preacher's exotic
bible thumping
redemptive hand waves.

I whip angel food
with the wood spoon
offer to capture the moon
make solace
tell her even a blind eye can be put right
as if there is a thornless version of happiness
I have eaten with a straight tongue
a magic recipe
while she is lost in the eucalyptus
mining the black night's tutelage.
As if nothing can be something
and something will be nothing
in the fatigable world.

You Don Your Rattleskin Shoes

don't stay
go off berserk
die of heart failure
enter that other dramatic realm.

The funeral is a glue gun affair against morbidity
too many angular ham and cheese sandwiches
dessert cakes, foil toothpicks
a sermon that negates your lonely hands
the terrain of sin the world rakes.

I ice feet
practice penitence
imagine you in your rattleskin shoes
stapled to heaven
even the butterfly wings in your hair
flappable now
rhinestoned to blaze.

My Mother Marries a Dwarf

confirms largeness on the world's small feet
no pretension
just her hips flagrant walk
through unsung roses
her eye that holds small things
finds the jewel inside the pod's bleeding.

They are happy all told
navigate minefields
build a house of larkspur
muddy feet, lemon deliberations.
She sings Rilke out in the rye field
he knits blue socks
for her feet's hoarse heels.
The yellow envelope of happiness
kneels at their bed.

Neighbors shake their head
close up their yard gate
my mother of the so much promise
becomes *the dank one*
with berserk shoes.

But she has found heaven
knows the sodden tongue
that plays there.

My Mother Threatens to Put an Earring in
Her Nose

start over.
I abhor the idea
spend hours trying to dissuade
tell her *it is self-mutilation*
you have a fine nose - spare it.
We settle on ear piercing
thirty-eight years old at the chain mall
jewelry counter trying to decide on amethyst
or garnets for her first pair.
But I'm already afraid it won't stop here.

How many holes can the ear stand
before it revolts she asks the clerk.
The clerk says plenty and I see
my mother calculating
she has always liked spectacle
dabs of glitter
the yanked up hem.

My mother says -
the moon has many holes
sucks the dark earth dry
tumbles it like a rock spinner
till everything burns.

You Climb the Stairway to Heaven

find God waiting
not cream puff perfect
or addicted to mowed lawns
a chain link fence
but messy, as the tabernacle
of the day's misplaced feet
the suet that lumbers away from the bread.
Your rayon low cut dresses come back
anxious for the flawed
white exuberance of your skin
the hourglass curves that make
a treason of the world's gold teeth
pin men's eyes
ask them to pray.

Removed from the shelves
of neatly jarred jam
from a sundown that finds you kitchen bound
moping other people's supper plates
you stalk the beach
the wind's loose tongue
gull screech
your bare feet a cradle
in and out of the waves.

Contrition

There is no cold wind
people slipped off to heaven
in a blue haze
disconsolate dungarees on a
chaste clothesline.
The woman anchors her skirt down
ruinous around men with too much
afternoon on their hands
the aim of no restitution
the chain of their gold
pocket watches trailing.
She will make no *Our Father*
Hail Mary in their name
nor berate her tongue for its torn
down allegiances.

Soon it will be midnight
the garden's estranged roses
will run around indecent
in their scented shoes.
The small wafered girl
will climb her way diligently
up toward the eye of God
who sees all our cowardice
and rewards the thistle—
the least of them
in the vast kingdom of beauty—
the right to grow riotous
tall and prickly
while so disavowed
in a lily-clad world.

In the Three Bear Cottage

my mother falls in love with her wings
doesn't need to travel so far
finds the foam in the day's heaving
as if desertion is a petrified tongue
an annotation between forgiveness
and lusting for heaven.

St. Jude never saved us
with his ivory robe, thin shoes.
We buttressed the house up with stick pins
curly cue pillows
three beds for the bears who would come in
late night, their bodies slurring.
In May, they'd trundle off to capture the first
of the choke berries.

Finally she built a nest here of sorts
stick gum and rush, candle wax, birch twigs
twined them together, made a home
softer than the tongues of men who
want to carry her body off each night
then migrate.

My mother hives with the honeybees.
Doesn't need to travel far anymore
clog her head with useless devotion.
Even in the midst of winter
her soaked wings gleam.

My Mother Casts a Dark Spell

over the earth's blue tongue.
It wasn't always like this
pitchforking the day
growing briars in the midst of
the world's delphinium.
Once it was a different place
sweet william, the convalescence of roses
the man taking her arm tentative
gentle as he saw her into nightfall
every day a fire stoked and fanned
cared for in the constancy of its flame.

But that was long ago
before zippered feet
before fence lines and guardrails
the metal bodies that carry us
the shrinking, the terrible shrinking
of the earth's green limbs.

I tell you it was a different place back then
my mother knew it
swirled her white camisole
among the groves of lupine
the forsythia's loose tongue.
You could hear the sun wake
arch its arms over the drowse of poppies
as if there are no dark spells
and the worst nightmare
is to let ourselves be lost
in this field.

On Watching the Skyward Commotion
of Sparrows

You clear a path to dissolution
stockpile moonlight, canned meat, mission soup
tell the dog to stay calm
the children not to weary.
Half of you has always been like this
a dangle of feet off the pond dock
your mind stapled to paint pots
a field of sheep
beyond the night meal
avalanche of jobs.

Does it take absence
a raw disposition to hold the moon
travel the distance it takes to capture oneself
move past the chalk walled garden
ledger of *yes* and *no's*
confirm the ascendency of your roses?

You clear a path to dissolution
haphazard.
Some say you snowballed your life
axe handled it away
tried to rebuild
like the house on a warped foundation
girl with an abject past
who must eat up the rain
walk thin footed through wet grass
glue happiness to a luckless day.

In the clear deliberation of morning
you have bird feather pasted to your wings
corrugated lamplight
believe you can fly

gather the love notes of children
float above the lust of men
dust kisses.

You want to be small then great again
a capillary of God's arm
the sinuous Bo tree
dissolved as sugar in tea water
want that nothing
emptiness
that conscripts a defeated being
to sail forth and lift.

My Mother Preempts God

builds a fortress in my imagination.
Nothing is foreign, displeases
she is not angry at my betrayals
does not close a blind eye over
the world's raking

becomes the antidote to sin
parable I can live by.
We lull in the field grass
graze with lupine.
I find lost words—
antiquarian   sorghum   sojourn
dine on millet
the spider's injunction to weave and spin.

I don't understand why others have abandoned her
raised the nuptial of the head above
the music of her summer feet.
When the dark comes
my mother's hands soothe
orphaned bread
the wolf in the field
turn the man with a spotty past
into the wild succulence
of blood red roses.

You Place Timidity Among the Three Sins

that won't save us.
I curve away from your arm
give up my voice with its pall-mall
crucifixions
weighted happiness that scoops
cake batter out of the bowl
rings a jangle of silver bracelets

become nothing again
liquid as river
the child's grape juice
body's non inflammatory
a slow motion past towing.

Look at the wind you tell me
how it caresses the sky
lays its tongue over every
round thing, seduces field grass
rattles dead leaves, shakes tree limbs
lullabies the earth into loving it
senseless.

I become wind
wordless, swift as lightning
inscrutable in my missionary hands
incendiary
resolute as things fall apart
slide back together again.

PART FIVE
Ordinary as Moth Wings

My Mother Tells Me to Lick my Lips

let the wind assail.
I resist her advice
box the pockmarks of my life
make them salient
as if I can turn a mean machine
bruteless.

Is it possible to let nothing assail
not the wind nor men nor my mother
with her scrubbing brush, silk kimono
mercurial hands?

I prevail over the cake batter's delirium
decommission my lips from the
attention of undependable men
lubricants, pink tints
let the air treason.

Aberrant warrior
parched lips on a parched day
my mother a synopsis of all
that is unfinished in me.

Someday I will conquer the moon I tell her.
Someday.

I Crush a Ladybug by Accident

remember your adage to *love all things*
am poor at this
fall down at the start
like so many things—jobs, marriage, family
that collapse or are given away.
The day breeds its own kind of machinery.
I remember how you always looked best
in your element out of doors
among the slug colonies and roses.
How the fierce tongue of winter
never tempted your betrayal.

When I think of love
it is a blue glove
tissue thin devotions
the notion of *forever*
forklifted away.

I bury the ladybug
so I can sleep at night
light a fire beneath the
world's steel grate
remember you
in whose hands
the moon wrote its most caustic homilies
who told me - *what you love*
can get pieced back together
if not here
then in that other life
we've been saved for.

The Art of Pronunciation

My father said these are called *ranunculus*
had me repeat it back to him
Ren un qu las.
I never learned to pronounce them
afterwards erased the prescribed name for things
memorized only their bodies' sheen
scent of the bloom, whether they were
tissue breathed, stalwart, or fleeting as sunset.
Did they have necks long or short
turn in a breeze or stay fixed.
The simple word *flower* could take on
a multitude of meanings
some were gorgeously whimsical, provocative
perishable as money
others strict minded
diminutive as a child's purse.
There were floozy lipped lavenders
silken scarlets
furrows of crimson with yellow eyed centers.
They took over my closet, anointed my body
girl in lavender prayer book
tulip yellow street shoes.

Nobody recognizes me anymore
the map of my hands vined over
no harsh words, pronunciations to deceive me.
My father's epistles muddied with rain.

This Altar

I creep down the stairs
try to find you
my nightgown billowing
the dark a reprieve from my past
an altar I might learn to live in.

They say *all things come to a blind heart*
as if erasure saves
unencumbered shoes can shuffle in mud
mitigate the world's crow feet
keep their sides gleaming.

I tell you I have drunk dissolution
with a voracious tongue
but you don't move there.

I walk on street pitch
imagine the world new again
your arms coming toward me
fluid as the stars' clear face

come to know there is nothing
I can do alone with my hands.

I Eat the Sunlight

to see if you are listening
but you are off base
in the elsewheres
my mouth bloody
my body a shimmer.

No flashlight to find you
teeth ground down
to fine dust
like my brother's ashes.

Who will conscript the moon
wed me in dissolution
my knuckles brassy pink
til the avalanche
of light
saves.

I have kissed every flower
even the thistle
the lightening rod of my hands
a conscription of magic
out of the blue day.

I Look Through the Eye of God

and the world turns myopic.
I have my metallic dress on
get pulled into the earth's
angular technology
as if hope never buttressed a fuse
can lay three cords of wood
let the girl who traipses down
the road of uneasy happiness
waxwing the moon
find the fire of her feet's stomping.

You corral light
litter envelopes with sheep, foil wings
capture stars for my bed, red insects
the coyote's coral cup of hunger
as if any old thing can save
and my ordinary shoes are just another
face of the miraculous
when I let my feet enter.

I enter.
Fur eclipsed
shiny as seal skin.
Keep me here wandering around
the milk maid's ancient prerogative
to squeeze and to sing.

It Was Not Out of Sin

I received you
but out of busted hope
hysteria scissored away
as coarse cotton.

Make me a wish
you tell me
as if life holds a certain
stalwart vengeance
a soul can still ransack heaven
with stunted wings.

This is not how I thought it would be.
Not how I thought it would be.
The earlier notions of God
failed me.

Rift with nothing
I enter your hem
sleep there.

The Proposition of My Father's Hand

hangs like a torn thumbnail
ivory fruit in a sour wind.

It is Saturday
I open curtains
let the light drizzle
imagine my life no longer
thin as the neck of cosmos
but piquant
littered with my dead mother
her sanguine wishes for me.

Amen

I give you permission to be here
cloaked in my body's love
the two of us dissolved as sugar cubes
in hot water.
Now I speak your name slowly
let it linger
know the world is a fleeting place
a momentary sliver between past and eternity
and this love is worth more than
a resolute tongue
enameled toe shoes.

Under the gaze of the night's clear eye
I have found my heart's desire
ample as milk thistle
flimsy as the long necks of cosmos
smoky as these lips
that willingly bend and sway in the wind
their lavender and purple twin folds
gleaming.

When My Mother's Army of Ants

overrode the world
with their pyramids of sand
infinite bundles of asphalt
she wondered at the calm of them
the way their tiny bodies
steeled themselves to accept big loads
how their voices shrank down from
the chorus of night angels.

Now there are tall buildings
everywhere, industrial servants
time with its watch clock bent
on tallying.
You puncture the skin of the skin
with your wrists bleeding.

The analog of sin repeats itself
like a worn dog.
Come. Sit. Stay.
Democracy—you say
everyone given the same chance.

You are the end of all hope
our anthem's bleeding.
It takes more than three cocks
in the morning
to reach this place.

I Look Through the Eye of God and the World turns Magenta

clears its throat
untangles arms
as if winter has left no deathtrap
no single parent's hysteria
the car starts first time
the road is no longer plagued
with black ice
welcomes our wheels.

I notice balsam wreaths tacked to front doors
the snow people of some child's intact imagination
light infested trees
paw prints of jack rabbit, possum, deer
that lead over the hills
inscriptions of love
that keep the sky from falling

keep the sky from falling.

In the Hour of Disinclination

when the birds are weeping my love for you
I map the world unsteady
graph it with sin, disinclination
the chagrin that comes from loving
what can't be ours.
The rufus red tail dismounts from your perch
the world slips out of my hands
lands in quagmire, marsh reed
the diamond cutter's rapt imperialism
as if what we are born into
becomes us
as of the silver spoon
or the coveter of silver spoons
for whom one grain of sand will not be enough
nor the inconsequential magpie
the perishable lady slipper
forlorn child.

My love slips off the white egret
of your camisole in dim light.
My hands worship
intent on finding the pallor of your skin
cleave to what you remain above money
above the proposition of sanctity
to scour what it sends.

Holy is the day of my love.
Holy the lost treachery of my hands.
I tear open the envelope
of your rapt allegiances.
Become meadow.

Let me lie here then
despised by the earth's industry

our savage rage
to engulf what we don't understand.

Winter comes
with its precipitous tongue
forklifts the snow
the memory of my mother's deathbed.

I Hallucinate the Night

till it waxwings the moon
and I am deathless again
no longer afraid to be eaten alive
or die like my mother
one imperceptible breath at a time
till my heart can't live here.

The night has no more secrets to shield
I am porous
as lemon cake
good cognac
the intractability of children
who love what they seize.

Sunday Afternoon

You teach me how to stir pudding
without blackening the pot
to mend socks
take a minefield and convert it
slowly into mole hills
that time is just a swinging door
surplus of hinges.

The porch glider keeps rust
from drifting
holds down my legs
my ambitions with their ragged flame
reminds me of the proposition
of idleness in a gold coated world.

All day I circumvent the sun
let the shadows eat me
til I am a dark salacious woman
with the satisfaction of pudding
on my lips
the secret of uncensored homilies.

The Soft Gloved Ministries

They gave me a quote
imbedded in fortune cookie
sanitary as hospital rooms
my life with all its windows
whitewashed
as if inevitability wears no torn thread
and I am *all grown up*
all grown up
and that means sensible
as pummeled cotton
girls with lust torn
out of their hair's wingtips.

I will be tepid
you think
a timecard puncher, clock keeper
calendar manager
minister of soft gloved technology
will not disappoint
languish in bed under a silk comforter
crumble crumble crumble
be glad of the day's pallor for me.

It is July
all things pleasured by the sun's
unparceled tongue
the cosmos, geranium, day lily
willing themselves back
not sanctimonious with pinned hems
but flavored

as good soup
decent lovers
the colors of the world
you arrest
my liquid imagination
scrupulous eye burning.

Your Table

is white as snow
battery powered
can go anywhere
even when the wind limps

rakes the leaves
hides in them
cup of mush in a
camouflage world.

In May when the ground
grows tapioca enough
to receive any seed
and the iris wills herself
back from death
you forage the forgotten world
not stereophonic
but dazed from winter's sharp tongue
caked with the ivy's green
mangled devotion

prop up your feet
look at me with your blue eye, say—
*so what will you make of your life
this time?*
as if I am a cat with six lives
no chipped past
tattered slippers
as if death is as ordinary as moth wings
predictable as winter
and your table is still white

stippled in the coral stained
tongues of dead camellia
and it can go any place
marry any season
like me.

You Set Me Free To Live Again

Maybe you know
I can't apostrophe
the moon anymore
keep stick pining the past
make it stay
neat as a parasol
with no rips.

There is blood on my hands
men's hasty deliberations
I want to marry the cross
but everything I love
keeps slipping.

I smudge ink up my arm
sculpt clay women
who lean on the wind's loose voice.
You hold the key to midnight
keep an encyclopedic eye
on the world.

I lick the sunlight
see if you are listening.

Acknowledgments

Grateful acknowledgement is made to the following literary publications in which some of these poems first appeared (in slightly different versions):

Alimentum: "My Mother Wears Her Empire Waist Dress and Tries to Reconjure Heaven"

the Aurorean: "Sunday Afternoon"

Cider Press Review: "My Mother Wears Her Sage Musk and rethinks Heaven," and "My Mother Wishes for Happiness Settles for the World's Tutelage of Rapt Machinery"

Comstock Review: "My Mother Married a Dwarf and Confirms Largeness on the World's Small Feet"

Gingko Tree Review: "For a Moment My Mother Triumphs Over Her Past, Makes an Altar of Moonlight," and "In the Shadow of my School Biology Class"

Haden's Ferry Review: "My Mother Becomes a Scholar but Gets Bored There," and "The World's Hypnotic Aerial Heart Gloating"

Harpur Palate: "Everyone Wanted Carnations That Year"

Iris: "Bandits Come and Remove My Mother's Body in the Night"

The Journal (England): "My Mother Swallows the Snowy Plover in Our Back Yard"

Lake Effect: "My Mother Casts a Dark Spell Over the Earth's Blue Tongue"

the minnesota review: "My Mother's Body Turns Traitor on Her"

Notre Dame Review: "My Mother Hears the Polyphony of the Sky Breathing and Unburdens her Tongue"

The Penwood Review: "My Mother Hobbles Salvation Out of Her Paten Leather Shoes"

Poetry Salzburg Review (Austria): "In the Arms of the Hexagon"

Prairie Schooner: "In the Three Bears Cottage My Mother Falls in Love with Her Nest Wings"

Solo Poetry Review: "Midnight Hairpins My Mother's Hard Shoes"

Sunstone: "In the Book of Beatitudes My Mother Finds Her Freedom Again"

Takahe (New Zealand): "My Mother Dons Her Rattleskin Muff for Heaven," and "My Mother Threatens to Put an Earring in Her Nose and Start Over"

Weber: The Contemporary West: "Who Says the Shattered House Can't Live Here Anymore"

Book Finalist *May Swenson Award*
Semi-Finalist *Crab Orchard Series in Poetry*
Finalist *Anhinga Poetry Prize*
Semi-Finalist *University of Wisconsin Press*
Finalist *Carnegie Mellon University Press*

Toni Thomas lives in Portland, Oregon. Her poems have been published in Austria, Spain, New Zealand, Canada, England, Scotland, and Australia. In the United States her work has appeared in over fifty literary magazines including *Prairie Schooner, North Dakota Quarterly, Hayden's Ferry Review, the Minnesota Review, Notre Dame Review, Poetry East*, and more. She has been twice nominated for a Pushcart prize, and won several awards. She has published sixteen collections of poetry and four books for children.

Her figurative clay sculptures have been shown in gallery exhibits in Portland and Chicago, displayed in literary magazines, and housed in private collections in the U.S. and England.

Her short documentary *One of Us* was shown at the Trans-ideology: Nostalgia festival in Berlin and at the Museum of
Contemporary Art in Taipei.

Since Toni loves to create and sits buried in reams of poems, manuscripts, clay figures and images….she likes to imagine all of them out in the world, swaying wild as the lupine.

tonithomaspoetry.com